Always New
Beginnings

Helena Ana Young

BALBOA.
PRESS

A DIVISION OF HAY HOUSE

Balboa Press books may be ordered through booksellers or by contacting:

Balboa Press
A Division of Hay House
1663 Liberty Drive
Bloomington, IN 47403
www.balboapress.com
1 (877) 407-4847

Because of the dynamic nature of the Internet, any web addresses or
links contained in this book may have changed since publication and
may no longer be valid. The views expressed in this work are solely those
of the author and do not necessarily reflect the views of the publisher,
and the publisher hereby disclaims any responsibility for them.

The author of this book does not dispense medical advice or prescribe the use
of any technique as a form of treatment for physical, emotional, or medical
problems without the advice of a physician, either directly or indirectly. The
intent of the author is only to offer information of a general nature to help
you in your quest for emotional and spiritual well-being. In the event you use
any of the information in this book for yourself, which is your constitutional
right, the author and the publisher assume no responsibility for your actions.

Any people depicted in stock imagery provided by Thinkstock are
models, and such images are being used for illustrative purposes only.
Certain stock imagery © Thinkstock.

Print information available on the last page.

ISBN: 978-1-5043-7655-6 (sc)
ISBN: 978-1-5043-7656-3 (hc)
ISBN: 978-1-5043-7663-1 (e)

Library of Congress Control Number: 2017903565

Balboa Press rev. date: 06/22/2017

Contents

Introduction

The journey that life offers has many surprises. It would appear that if we love God and do what we are taught to do, our lives should be very good and blessed. Times of trouble should be over as we live for the Lord. First lesson—this is not so. In fact, trouble is God's willing tool. From the day we come into the world in body, we are given rites of passage. Learning to crawl was really bothersome, but that was surpassed when walking was the task. And so on goes the pattern of humankind. Some are easy and quick learners to live tasks while others, like me, have to have the hammer hit and with a scream ask the question, "Why me, God?" We are taught that survival and "fitting in" are the most important things a human can do from the time we are small until we become conscious that there is more to life than these two things. This inner consciousness comes through many trials and tribulations, many tears, and many screams. God, what do you want? God, why did this happen to me?

God, where were you when I needed you? There are also the cries of the Spirit within, which longs to escape its silence, but the many messages in our thinking keep us prisoners to our bodies. The messages have been there from the beginning of our indoctrination into society. And so the ego grows. The messages the ego has to deal with are mostly the problems of the body. What are we to eat? What are we to wear? What are we to drive? Who will love me? When we feel we are on the outside looking in, we continually strive to be what others want us to be. This cycle continues until we come to the end of our delusion and wake up. There has to be more to life than existing. Without the experience of awakening, we continue to walk in darkness, all the time thinking we know what we are doing. God is in the heavens, and we are on earth. Never the two shall meet.

The reason I have written my life story is to encourage. We all are alive with the life of the Creator, which is in you, for from Him and to Him are all things. This means all of us. We have come to earth to have a human experience to lead us into a heavenly experience. There are marvelous things that can happen to you if you can realize the wonder of this. I invite you and challenge you to expand your vision and see that there is more to you than a body.

My Beginning

*B*eing born to parents who had their own problems is not the best way to come into the world. Mom was from upper Minnesota and had been raised there— or perhaps I should say she *existed* there. Her mother had diabetes and tuberculosis and had to live in a tuberculosis facility for a long time. Grandmother died in Mom's arms when Mom was only a small girl. Mom also had a peach of a father who was never there. He would go to town to play cards. There were ten other children, of which two girls were farmed out to relatives hundreds of miles away, leaving the boys at home to work in the fields. The boys worked hard and played hard. Only one of them escaped alcoholism. Mom said they would always play pranks on her, like scraping on the house and growling, pretending to be a bear. Mom had to leave school and take care of the family after her mother died, as she was the oldest girl. She was given gunnysacks for dresses, and she would put a hole in the top for her head and in the middle for her arms. She then sewed them as well as she could, but she was never a good sewer. She was a skinny little thing—only ninety pounds fully grown. It did not take long before salesmen came around, along with the mailman and others who knew that Grandpa was in town playing cards. With the boys in the fields, the opportunity was open to satisfy their needs with Mom. Mom was devastated, and there was no one to share her panic and pain. Her life was not pleasant. She was a survivor, but she was hurt psychologically for the rest of her life.

Dad was left after his mother passed away when he was just a child. Grandpa did not marry again, but no one knows just why. Grandpa was a stoic, big Swedish man who had worked hard and acquired a large farm. That was a sign of wealth in those days. He was a controlling man who did not show emotions. Instead of hugs, Dad was given whatever he wanted, so I was told, and he was not taught to be responsible. He lived on the wild side and enjoyed his freedom. This made life for my mother frustrating because she never knew if bills were paid. Dad loved Mom, however, and stuck it out throughout their life together. I remember how he was there for her in all her illnesses.

How their lives were woven together is a wonder, but when Mom was a young woman, she was hired out to be a housekeeper for my Grandpa. It only took one look and my father was in love with Mom. He informed his dissatisfied father, who was looking to marry him to a wealthy neighbor's daughter, that he was going to marry this woman, my mom, and so it was.

Now, into this wonderful family a boy was born, whom Grandpa dearly loved, and then later a girl arrived. That was me. My brother had all the small features of my mother, and I got my features from my father, who was also a big man. Once a week Grandpa would open his coin purse and announce that he was going to give some money to the kids. Charles, my brother, would get quarters, and I would get pennies. Boy, did that make me feel important. But then women were not worth too much, except to cook, clean, wash, and iron clothes. And of course married women had to satisfy their husbands. What a future I had to look forward to—a free housekeeper. Everything in me rebelled at that thought.

I don't know what was going on in my brain before I was born, but I didn't want to come out into the world and so I wiggled and resisted enough inside that belly until I had wrapped that cord around my neck several times. When I was forced to leave my happy, warm home, I came out blue and refusing to breathe. What an entrance! Everyone was shaken up but looked happy that I was there. And later when Dad went to register me, He called me Helena, but his nickname for me was Snookie. Yuck! I didn't have a chance in life; I was destined to be a big kid with a gap between my front teeth. Who wants to be a friend to a big, cross-eyed girl with permanent frizzy hair and a gap between her front teeth?

Mom told me of the time Grandpa was having a beer in the basement, and I came down to get some canned goods. Grandpa called me over and gave me a drink out of his bottle. I have always liked the taste of beer even when I was just five, but Mom was outraged because Grandpa brought me upstairs drunk. I don't remember this, but Mom told me that I should be careful because I liked beer too much.

My childhood memories are not pleasant. Mom was always sick or in the hospital because she needed some surgery or something else was happening. She had inherited a poor body, and she was suicidal with thoughts that her life had too many horrible things happen in it and she was not good enough to live anyway, as Grandpa informed her often. One day she wanted to die and was headed to the swamp to drown herself. I, at six years of age, was hanging on to her leg, and she dragged me along. I was trying to hold her back, crying and screaming for Dad to come. He finally heard my screams and came running to rescue her. I look back today and now understand why she was so unhappy and nervous. She never felt good enough and spent most of her life trying to please everyone, but it was never enough. Everything in the house had to be perfect, and the food, including baked goods, had to be the best to please my grandfather. I had to wash and wax the living room floor every Saturday, even though no one was allowed in there except when company came. Mom's need to be loved was overwhelming, and she took me, as her daughter, to pour her life story into. She needed someone to talk to, and even though I was young, she told me stories about her life and her cousins in Sweden and things she wanted in life. She loved to dance and would imagine herself as a great dancer, dressed in beautiful gowns while floating across the floor. Her desire for beauty was all over her, and even though she did not get all the beautiful things she loved, she taught me to love beautiful things like music and dancing.

She was hospitalized for a whole year after she had a nervous breakdown. I was never told how long she would be in the hospital or what happened, where, and why she was taken. We kids were never allowed to visit her. These were hard and confusing times for me. There was a time when I was farmed out to my aunt and uncle's home. There was only one upstairs bedroom with two big beds, and we all slept upstairs. There was no bathroom inside the house; there was only a *pissapotin* (a pot to pee in) upstairs in that room that was used at night. During the day we had to use the outside toilet, which scared me as I thought a snake could crawl up and bite me while I was using it. Talk about learning to potty quickly. No wonder I have had problems. I was told by my aunt that my uncle walked in his sleep so I shouldn't be scared, which of course scared me every night. At her house, I had to clean and take care of the baby. The biggest joy of my life was the cat. Baby was a fat angora that cuddled and purred and gave me the comfort and love that I longed for. I also was rewarded by a wonderful piece of pie or a cinnamon bun or some other scrumptious sweet. Food became the way I took care of my hurting heart. Comfort food was good and did the job temporarily.

Several months later, I had to go back home because there was no one to do the housework there, so I became the cook, cleaner, clothes washer, and ironer—basically everything a woman was expected to do. I was eight years old at the time. Memories of good times include playing cards with my grandpas and my brother, climbing the shed, teasing the bull, running in the fields, biking, standing on the stoop in the yard, and singing. My brother was always with the men except those times when we were with the two grandpas playing games, mostly cards. I was an active kid with tons of energy, and my father would catch me, put me in his crossed legs, and hold me there until I would simmer down. My father was a tease and was always playing some trick on my brother and me. I was deathly afraid of frogs. I used to scream every time I saw a frog in the basement, where we had to go to the bathroom. Mother thought I was hurt and came running every time I screamed. Dad was given the job of helping me overcome my phobia. He caught a frog and offered me one dollar to carry it to my mother. With much hesitation I did it, but it didn't solve the problem. I just tried not to scream loudly from then on when I saw a frog. Frogs and snakes are not a blessing to me.

Music, especially Metropolitan Opera of the Air, was a big part of my good times. I listened intensely every Saturday and let my imagination soar to the drama of the music. My brother used to poke fun of me because I loved opera music. Hoity toity was the name he called me, but I continued to listen, lost in its beauty. Mom played the accordion and piano, so each time one of the relatives came over, we would gather around the piano and sing hymns. Mom always wanted to show me off, and I had to sing several songs. I felt so good when I was told how good I sang.

It seemed that every time a relative came to see us, I was told, "Oh, how big you've gotten" Those words stuck in my thinking, and I looked at myself and looked at the other girls in school and saw that I indeed was about a foot or more taller than the other girls. I also saw that I wore glasses because I was cross eyed and I had two front teeth that were far apart, and at eight years of age, I began to have breasts. What a mess! Apparently there was something wrong with my growth hormone that caused me to develop early. Oh, how I wanted to be small like the other girls. I was not popular and was always the last person picked on the teams. I attended a country school that had only about twenty-four students and there were only two other girls in my class, and they were small and cute. My life sucked!

Another thing that shook my world was when another aunt and uncle joined a Pentecostal church in Minneapolis and would drive each Sunday to this church. My cousins, the cute little girls, got "saved," and when I stayed overnight, they would try to get me "saved. They spoke of hell and fire if I did not give my life to God. They scared the life out of me! I was left at this church one Sunday when Dad went to see Mom. It felt very warm and cuddly, and there was a lot of singing. People raised their hands and danced and shook all over. They seemed to be having a good time with God. I did not understand what was going on. I felt good, scared, and excited at the same time. God was a real pull on my heart even though I was afraid of Him. They had asked Dad to come to the service, but he said he couldn't because the devil might corner him there. We never went back.

One of the most outstanding things happened to me when I was out riding my bicycle. I was riding down a hill in the wind when all of a sudden, I was engulfed in a vale of clouds. There was so much peace and love in that cloud that I could hardly breathe. A light surrounded me, and I began to cry. They were tears of joy, love, and fear. I was afraid because I didn't know what it was. It kind of reminded me of the feeling I had in my cousin's church. This same feeling of joy and love has followed me all my life. Whenever I need peace, I think of that cloud, and I am covered again. I never told a soul about this experience because I was afraid they would think I was crazy. It was only after several years that I had a moment of enlightenment and came into understanding that I knew what the cloud was and why it was given to me to experience.

Now I had a cat, God, and Mom also, when she came home from hospitals. Whenever she was there, I was told that it was my job to care for her, and I quickly developed into a great caretaker. Dad was always there working on the farm, and he often went into the garage and came back smelling of alcohol. I liked the smell. I never saw Dad drunk that I can remember, but I knew he liked to take a nip now and then. He was a big, strong man who could lift a car to change a tire. I was in awe of him but never got too close because he was always busy on the farm. As a young girl, there wasn't anyone I could confide in, so I lived in my own thoughts, pretending, standing on my sawed-off tree trunk, singing with my heart, and dreaming.

I had developed early at age eight because of a glandular problem, and I looked like I was eighteen. We attended the wedding of one of my cousins when two of her groomsmen began to hit on me, not knowing how old I was. It was frightening to me at that age, but I was frightened and also excited. For Christmas that year, I received two presents—a baby doll and my period. Talk about a paradox.

After a year in the hospital, Mom came home with

the news that she had to get away from the farm and
my grandfather or she would not get well, so they
decided Montana looked good. Dad went first and
got a job in the Anaconda copper smelter. We took a
train later, and as I looked at all the huge mountains
and viewed things I had never seen, the wonders of
the world opened new understandings. Montana was
a good place to land, we were in the mountains above
the world. I went to junior high school and high school
there. My dad worked in the smelter where they melted
the copper. It was hard work, and he was gone a lot.
Mom also was good enough physically, and she got
a job in the hospital. She had always wanted to be a
nurse and was delighted to work in a hospital. For me
this was junior high age, and I wanted to be liked and
have fun. Movies were open on Saturdays, and all the
kids would find a partner and make out. Not too many
saw the entire movie, but the libido that flowed was hot
and heavy. There was a big skating rink across from
the school, and the kids would go there each weekend
to have fun. I went to skate there even though I was
not too good at it. One day I fell, and before I could
get up, a big boy got on my back and kept pushing me
down and laughing. My back was wounded, and I was
hospitalized and had to lie on a board for three days
before I could walk. I didn't return to the skating rink.

Chapter 2

Beginning to Grow

*M*y self-image had not changed, and I always felt out of place all through those school years. I just did not fit in. I had physically developed, which opened up the door for me to fit smoothly into the drinking world. I could go into bars and never was carded. I also could go into liquor stores to buy the booze. 1 had a friend who thought like me, and together we made our way through these teen years, partying and drinking. She was an American Indian whose mother had passed, and her father had married a white woman who knew nothing of her culture. Her father died, leaving her with a stepmother who was like an old maid. She was not happy and did not fit with the school crowd, but we both fit together into the bar scene. I would buy the beer for the drinking crowd. This gave me the opportunity to drink, and I did. I was *not* a good drinker, and when I reached a certain point, I would remember the God who was in charge of hell and would flip out, screaming and crying and running. No one was interested in what I was doing because they were busy with their own good times, and they thought I was crazy anyway.

There was a sexy-looking older man I teamed up with. He had gotten back from the Korean War and was ready to have a good time. We went drinking at a bar, and of course, I drank too much and had to be carried into the house. Dad was working the night shift; Mom was in the hospital for surgery, so I was alone. I thought no one would know I had been drinking so, I went to bed, but the next morning when Dad came home, he followed the smell of booze right into my bedroom, woke me, and asked, "Who were you with last night because I am going to kill him?" Needless to say, the sexy man disappeared when I told him what my dad said. So much for love!

I also went through a phase that demanded that I look perfect, so daily I prepared my clothes, ironing, polishing, and making sure every hair was in place. I looked good. I was teased for this by the boys. There were boys who wanted to get in my pants and were making bets about who would do it, but I was too self-conscious to let anyone see my body. "When I get a figure like Marilyn Monroe, I will have sex with you," was always my response.

I was always getting involved with the wrong crowd and was always helping them with their love problems. I had crushes on the ones who were the worst. It seemed I was destined to love those lost ones and would end up alone and heartbroken because they always went somewhere else for love. This broke my heart many times, so I hid my feelings in my weekend parties. One positive blessing—I was still a virgin.

I always loved music and would sing solos for school concerts and other things. Singing was my one strong point. The school participated in an all-state music competition. I was entered to sing, and to my surprise, the rating of the song I sang was superior. The judges all agreed that I had to make music and singing my career. They stated that I was a natural. I was in seventh heaven, thrilled, and delighted, and this set my life in motion to go to music college. At last there was something I could do that would make me feel accepted.

Chapter 3

Beginning to Learn

$\mathcal{M}$y college years were full of parties. I, of course, fell in love with one of the teachers, James. He was in love with a married woman who was not happy in her marriage but was not willing to leave her husband. However, she was willing to meet James and have a good time with him every once in a while. On those days James was in heaven and I was in hell. Meanwhile, I spent every minute I could with him. Almost all through my college, James was in my life. We were inseparable. James was in a band, and every Saturday night I was at the dance hall watching him play, drinking, and falling in love with the music, the big band sound. When James had to go into the army, I followed him to the town where he was stationed and where he played in the army band. James wanted me always near and available but did not love me romantically. I was a pal. I would have lost my virginity if he had given me half of a romantic look. While he was stationed in that town, he ended up getting a girl pregnant and had to marry her. He returned to my house because this girl had to be hospitalized, and we drank together in my apartment. James and I sat on the living room floor of my apartment surrounded by booze and got drunk. When she was released from the hospital, James left with her, and I never saw or heard from him again.

After James left my life, I started to join different singing groups. I joined a church that had an excellent choir. The director was quite famous for his excellent leadership in choir music, and I sang music that was so very wonderful. I did a lot of singing when I was in college and thought that one day I would be a Wagnerian opera star. I studied, practiced hard, and tried to put my life into music. I was still a party girl and found people who sang in the choir who loved to have a party too. We hung out every weekend and would go to dinner and afterward would have drinks and fun late into the night. I decided I would be like Auntie Mame after I saw the movie and bought a cigarette holder that was about a foot long and bought dresses that were soft and swishy. I was introduced to the gay crowd as I was bar hopping with my friend.

There were so many talented gay men who loved beautiful things. They could design the most beautiful clothes and were always up for something thrilling. I would go regularly to gay bars with one of the guys. They loved my singing, and I would belt out an aria from some opera. I became the belle of the ball. I was popular, and that felt good.

One weekend the church I attended sponsored a retreat in the lake area. After attending some of the groups, which were boring, we came up with the idea that there had to be some excitement somewhere, so off to town we went to find something that would liven up the party, like firecrackers. There were people ice fishing on the lake. There were all kinds of cars and fish houses on one part, which made the lake look very enticing. It didn't take long for all of us to agree that a spin on the lake in the car would be just what we needed. It was so much fun. The car spun as we raced toward the other side of the lake.

Suddenly I saw water and asked, "What is that?"

Too late! The front of the car broke through the ice, and the car started to sink into the depth. Everyone but me could swim and exited the car quickly. The doors in the back shut, and the front end was going down deeper and deeper. Alone, I drew up my feet so they wouldn't get wet and thought, *I guess this is my end. I am going to die.* But the thought didn't stay, and I thought at least I had to try to get out. I began to open the window, and the water started to pour into the window. I was wet but determined to get out. I was in heavy winter clothes, which were bulky and big. Winters are cold! I stood up on the seat and tried to stick my head out the window, but the water was coming in full blast. Suddenly I felt hands around my waist holding me tight, and they began to move me up and out of the window. Those hands held me all the way to the shore. On the shore I kneeled down and thanked God for saving my life. I was so grateful!

"God, I'll do anything you want me to."

Soon all my friends were back together. We all looked like drowned rats freezing from the swim. The firemen who rescued us from the cold looked at the submersed car and shook their heads. How did we escape death? Five minutes more and we could all have been dead. It was truly a miracle. We were taken to the hospital, checked out, and released to head back to the retreat. We decided to celebrate our miracle, and so the next night when everyone could make it, the booze flowed. We all laughed at the event that almost took our lives.

Where was God? He seemed to be around when I was in trouble, but He was always hidden somewhere, and my mind was too full for too much of God. I was busy, however, in church because it had a wonderful choir and I was happy getting to know the members, especially those who partied. I remember going to sing on a Sunday so hungover that I could hardly make it up the aisle. I was a party girl, and every Sunday I would come with something new to shock everyone. I really was able to hide how insecure I felt, pretending I was the belle of the ball. With my long cigarette holder, I fit into the gay scene very easily, and they were very happy to take me on as their prodigy. I was wined and dined by the most wonderful men, who were creative and wildly imaginative. God was not on my mind very much. There was one time that I felt I was being called by God and went to the pastor of the church to understand what this was that I was feeling.

He listened and said, "Don't worry. You have had a lot going on, and this will pass. Just get on with your life's plans."

I look back on my life now and see that all the way the Spirit was just waiting to get me in the right place and time. Outward appearances, dresses and shoes, and beads and bangles were for me, and of course, I was a singer who should dress in this way! Life was looking good—except for those times when I felt I was still an empty nothing.

Chapter 4

Beginning to Expand

$\mathcal{N}$ew York—what a wonderful town, a town to really get lost in. And I was that girl who, with wide eyes, came to find my future. There are so many places to go and things to do in New York. Studying was not on my agenda of importance. I had a good voice and was asked to sing in many places, even being a guest singer for the Messiah, with orchestra, which was the thrill of a lifetime. There was still something missing, however, and I did a lot of pretending to fit in, knowing I still was not small and pretty like other women. I watched other women sing who were so beautiful and was green with envy. Outside I looked fashionable, but inside I was hurting terribly. I was alone and lonely even when I was in a crowd.

I was studying an opera on a Sunday afternoon,

enjoying the singing, especially the bass singer. He had one of the most beautiful voices I had heard. As I was enthralled in what I was hearing, I was interrupted by a man who appeared to be someone who was not upright.

"Are you enjoying the opera?" he questioned.

"Get lost," was my reply, and he left.

After the opera was over and I was preparing to leave, he approached me again. "Would you like to meet the singers?" he asked.

I was very surprised that he would know them, so I accepted the challenge, and sure enough, he did. Henry, the bass, was very open, and immediately we became friends. Henry asked Richard if he could entertain me until 9:00 p.m. as he had an appointment that had to be kept, and Richard agreed. "I'll take her to church."

That seemed to be okay as I was used to going to church, big, beautiful, and unique ones that had elaborate singing and beautiful surroundings. Off we went. I had never been on a subway before, so I didn't know where we were going, and when it came to the end of the line for us, we descended to the street. It was hell! There were people standing and nodding, others scurrying fast to get somewhere else. I then became aware that I was the only white person in the area.

I was in Spanish Harlem. I had never seen anything like this and was scared, but Richard hurried me off to the church. It was an old four-story building in the middle of the block. We went up the stairs into a room filled with people who were singing and swaying to the music that was playing. Their hands were in the air as they sang, and often there was a hallelujah, praise God, and some funny gibberish and a shaking of the head. What in the world was going on? Finally, the pastor stood up and spoke in Spanish, and the people sat down. The pastor looked straight at me and Richard and in English asked Richard to introduce me. I was flabbergasted and embarrassed to be pointed out, and then he asked me to give a testimony. My mind was dizzy. I had never been in this predicament, but I stood up shaking and said I was there because Richard had brought me there and quickly sat down. After the service was over and it was time to meet Henry, we left, with me briskly telling Richard off.

"These people are crazy. How dare you bring me to such a place?"

It was very confusing because there was a memory that I had from when I was a child in a church where people did the same thing, and I didn't understand it then and did not want it.

Henry and I began to practice and sing together.

25

Henry taught me how to relax my throat while singing, and he gave me lessons whenever we could get together. Henry belonged to a group of people who were taking drug addicts into their group, trying to rehabilitate them through exposure to the fine arts. It did not take long before I was friends with the whole group and hung out with them whenever I could. It seemed like a wonderful thing for people to do to help those poor guys who were addicted to drugs.

One evening I was asked to accompany a friend to a meeting to save Riverside Hospital Detox Unit, which was a hospital that would detoxify heroin addicts and then return them to the streets. They thought it was a waste and were there to listen to the other points of view. My friend told me, "When this is over, we'll go have dinner and drinks," so I agreed and stood by as they all talked. When the meeting was over, I was standing by the window waiting when a short, fat woman came waddling up to me.

She looked me straight in the eyes and said, "Young woman, when I was coming up in the elevator, God spoke to me and told me to tell you that you are called and wanted in His service."

My heart dropped. "Who are you to say this to me?" I asked.

She quickly pulled out a photography book and

began to show me pictures of her work. She said her husband and she had a church in the Bronx and were working with drug addicts. I recognized the church in the picture. Unbelievable—she was the pastor of the church that had all the craziness going on, and I remembered the embarrassment I felt. Quickly, I excused myself and made my way to my friend. When we were in the club eating, I told her about the incident, laughing, but she was serious and spoke of Sister Leo very highly. "She is a real leader in the community." I shut up and we went on drinking.

I was fascinated by all the things that were in New York and would walk around just looking at all the stuff that was available. I found a job with a Japanese import company, which exposed me to the styles and culture of Japan. I ate sushi for the first time, saw how precious silk was made and marketed, and ended up leaving the job sooner than I really should have, but other plans were in the wind.

Life has a funny bone, and after several months Richard came to visit me. It just so happened that at the time I was going through papers looking for my college transcript. There was my church membership with the list of what constituted our doctrines.

Richard picked it up, read it, and stated, "My pastor would love to see these."

My mind went to Sister Leo and egotistically thought, *I'll show her.*

"Take them and show them to her, and also take my college transcript to show her that I *was not* someone she could fool."

He left with all the documents, and I did not see or hear from him for months. The time came for me to register at Julliard and I needed my transcripts and remembered that I had given them to Richard. I felt angry at his lack of concern and determined to take care of the situation myself, but I had to build up my courage.

Chapter 5

Beginning a New Life

With a lot of anxiety and fear, I took the subway up to the Bronx and walked down the streets to the church. Climbing the stairs, past the chapel, and up another flight, I was about to knock on the door when it flew open, and there she stood.

"I've been waiting for you," she said.

My heart dropped as she took me into the living room, sat me at the table, and began to talk. She talked and talked, telling me all about her life and how God had called her at a very early age and everyone thought she was crazy because her whole family belonged to a church that did not believe that God could speak. She had gone through persecution, and while praying for strength, God had given her a vision of people caught in a big hole who could not get out no matter what they did.

"Go and tell them the way, and help them get out of the hole," God told her.

That was how she came from Puerto Rico to New York, married, and began to work with the addicts. She whipped out her photographic book and showed me her first victory, Joe, and I could see her pride and happiness about his change. She went on and on until it was about four in the morning and I was still there. She insisted that I was not to go out and must stay the rest of the night because it was not safe for me at this hour.

In the morning, I quickly dressed and was on my way out, but while going past the chapel, I stopped and went in. Something had happened to me, and I had to know the truth. I had never heard the things Reverend Leo spoke about. A God who speaks and shows you what He wants—either this was crazy or it was real. I didn't know what God was all about.

I went to the altar and said to God, "If You are real, I want to know it. I will make a deal with You: for one week I will not drink, smoke, or go to parties but will do what I think Christians do."

I started my quest because I was stirred by what had been said and really wanted to know if this was just craziness or if it could be real. On the third day, in the subway, I found out God was real. I was taken out of the subway, in my mind, to a plateau that was higher, and there a voice spoke to me about the life I was living. My hidden fears were all exposed. I was totally confused and heartbroken and crying so hard that my mascara was all over my face. How could I live so long and not know God is real? I knew that I needed to do something but did not know what. I ran to the church in the Bronx and to Sister Leo. I sat in the chapel for a long while, and I was still crying when she came in.

Looking at my face all stained with tears, she asked, "What's wrong, honey?"

I answered, "I'm a sinner and a fake."

She said, "I know, honey." And she turned and walked away.

I followed her upstairs still crying, and that was the beginning of a new walk. There was a God. I was received with open arms and told again that I was chosen by God for a ministry. She spoke of the first time she had seen me on the elevator and the words that were spoken to her. She said I needed to come to Damascus and live for a while so I could be trained.

I moved into Damascus, bag and baggage. The day I moved into the church, I carried two pieces of luggage up the stairs at a time. With each trip that I took up, someone was carrying them down the fire escape and out onto the street. I was left with one little hand case that had two blouses and makeup. There were no skirts or dresses or any essentials. I had nothing! Sister Leo took me into the bedroom and began to go through her clothes and take out what she thought would fit me. Everything was big and needed to be taken in. Everything was also black or brown or dark blue. She said these were colors that were necessary for someone who was in ministry. I accepted this as part of the training I had to have. I took everything that was required as training, no jewelry, no tight skirts, no makeup, no swimming, no movies, no worldly music, and last, no cutting my hair. Reverend Rosado was pretty firm on me because I was a Swedish girl in a Spanish church surrounded by men who were drug addicts. Even though most of the men had given their hearts to God, they still were men, and I was a girl of eighteen years—dumb!

Someone once said that I was so green you could stick your hand through me, and I would have to agree. I got in so many situations that could have been disastrous had not God watched over me. I fell for one of the guys, and he went back to using and left. After several months, I got a call from him saying he needed me. Wow! I hurried down to where he was in a hotel and was told that he was out of money and had to move because he and another guy had been robbing all the rooms and the stuff was in his room. He couldn't just leave because they would find the stuff and he would be arrested.

Coming to his rescue, I said, "Let's put the stuff in your partner's room. That way you can just leave." So we did, and when I was finished, he said, "Gee, thanks," and went the other direction from me. If we would have been caught, I would have gone to jail. Dumb! Learning is hard and sometimes very hurtful.

The governor of Puerto Rico had heard about me, and I received an invitation to sing on the capitol steps for Easter. I stayed in Puerto Rico for six months at the home of one of Sister Leo's friends. I traveled the island singing and giving testimony of my salvation. There was a young man who had been in the services where I was singing who wanted me to go out with him. He was cute, and this was very exciting to me. When I spoke to Reverend Rosado, he looked at me so sternly and asked if I wanted to be called a harlot. I got upset at this as I was eighteen and had been making my own decisions for a long time. How dare he insinuate that I shouldn't go out with him. He said I could not go anywhere alone with this young man but I could go for coffee with him if someone went with me. Learning the customs of other nationalities was also hard. During this time, I ate a banana split daily and had gained twenty pounds, and the few clothes I had were kind of tight. Back in New York after I got new clothes, I began to sing in many church services, even for other ministries that worked with drug addicts. Converts who testified that they were saved from drugs brought in money that was needed. For ten years I followed the teaching and training of the church. I also went to Bible school.

Bible school was a real trip. There were so many cute girls there who seemed to fit in very well. I loved God so much that I was able to keep to myself and do the things required. I never felt accepted by the administration of the school, who were very appropriate for that atmosphere. I only knew God from the streets, and He loved the addicts. It seemed that fitting in meant that the addicts should stay in their corner and not intermingle with me or the others. I spent most of the time fasting and praying, studying, and going to other churches to sing and give testimony of my marvelous conversion. I decided that I would do a forty-day fast. I needed all the gifts of the Spirit to heal the addicts. At lunch and dinner times, I would go to the prayer room and on my knees beg God to give me the gifts to heal the world, and I would not hear the answer coming. I did have good times crying and praising. On the thirty-ninth day, I finally got a message.

"When you walk in the fruit, the gifts will be there when you need them." What a joker God is. I had to go through the thirty-nine days to humble myself and realize I knew nothing. God was knocking open my pride.

Sister Leo would come to the school several times a year and bring addicts with her so they could see that they could go to school and study for the ministry. These were great times for me because I was so proud of the work and wanted everyone to see that God was healing addicts and calling them to the ministry. I felt that this was what I was called to do and so I tried to put a passion in the rest of the students for this ministry

During my senior year, I was asked to create an hour program for the rest of the school. After much prayer, I was hit by the fact that no one there was acquainted with the lives people led on the streets of New York. It came on me like a dream, and pretty soon I had written a play that depicted the life of an addict. It was called *No Hope*, because that was the message each addict had. Once an addict, always an addict. In order to act out the part of the addicts, I decided I would ask the addicts who were in the program, my addicts, to play the parts I had written. It didn't take them long to learn the parts because they had lived the life. Each scene would end with whispers of, "No hope" because nothing was able to help them change. The final scene ended with the addict on his face on the floor calling out to God for help, and softly the music started with the song "Whispering Hope" being played until the addict surrendered to God and was changed. The play was a complete success. We were invited to put the play on in New York at Hunt's Point Palace, which was also a great success and with a packed-out crowd.

We took the play on the road with all the players after I was finished with school, to raise money for the work. Traveling from church to church and from stage to stage brought in money, but it was never enough. Soon we decided to take it on the road to different states also. This was an eye opener for me when one day while I was driving the van, I looked over to see Frankie with tears flowing down his face.

I asked him what was wrong and he said, "I have never been out of New York! I have never seen green grass and trees, and it's so beautiful."

I sat amazed. There are people who never do get out of the city, who never have the chance to see the world—people who think that every place is brick and buildings, subways and filth. How humbled I became and grateful that I had lived in many states. I had seen the mountains and the ocean, and it really didn't mean anything to me. I had taken for granted that which everyone should have the opportunity to experience but couldn't because of the circumstances of their lives. Another thing that shocked me as we visited church after church was how different they were. Some would not allow you to wear any jewelry, some asked me to wear dark clothes, and some were just creepy, but there were some that filled my heart and we all rejoiced at that time. Offerings were small as most churches took a part for their work.

I traveled with the guys for almost a year and then decided to go back to the ministry and start teaching and begin to try preaching. Teaching came very easy as I knew I had that gift from God and was confident in the messages of the Bible. But preaching was very difficult, as I was full of fear that I was not good enough and therefore when given a chance to preach ended up speaking for about ten minutes, and Sister Leo had to finish the message. She took off on what I started, and I sat embarrassed with my head down as in prayer. I thought for that time that my ministry was to sing, teach, and testify. I did not give up on preaching, however, and little by little began to understand that real preaching was sharing the message of your heart and did not depend on the proper forms learned in school. Bloopers and accidents, which I have had, stay in the minds of some of my dearest friends, and we often laugh at the things that have made their way out of my mouth. Thank God I know I am just another human and can laugh at my inability to speak perfectly. Speaking has been one of my greatest blessings, both to me and to others. I often have people come up to me and tell me what they remember of messages I have given. It blows me away!

One day Reverend Rosado asked me to drive the men up to the house that they had bought for the men to stay while they were looking for God. There were eight men plus groceries that had to be brought up for the guys who were still there. The transportation was an old, dilapidated airport limo that had been repaired by Reverend Rosado, who thought he was a mechanic. He was not.

The building was located in the Catskill Mountains, which meant there were sharp turns as we gradually ascended to reach the top. There were the men, all very dark skinned, and me, a very white Scandinavian blondie. Also in the back of the car were bags of rice and beans, the favorite, and other daily food. As I approached a sharp curve and put on the brakes to slow down, there were *no* brakes. I turned the steering wheel away from the edge of the mountain, only to find *no* steering, and I screamed, "God help!"

The car stopped so fast that I hit my body on the wheel. I and all the guys sat dumbfounded for a while. Everyone was okay—a bit shocked but thanking God. A short time later, a highway patrol came by, stopped, looked over us, and asked, "What the hell are you guys doing?"

I explained who I was and where I was taking the guys, and he began to look over the situation very suspiciously. After looking the car over inside and outside, he turned to me and asked, "Why are you still alive? This limo should be at the bottom of this mountain."

I told him that I had cried out to God and that God had answered. He just shook his head and called for help. We found out that the axle had broken in the middle, and it really was a miracle that we were alive. That limo had seen its day. We all shouted our thanks to God. Wow, that was scary. That was the second time my life was saved by a miracle. God be praised.

About this time, I met a funny guy and fell in love right away. He was an ex-drug addict who had a ministry of healing. He was fun, romantic, good looking, sexy, and just wonderful. He could have been a model because he was tall and thin besides good looking. We were soon an item, and the relationship went from romantic lovers to married partners. Our wedding was held in the church with Sister Leo performing the service. Sister Leo had made my wedding dress. She also planned the reception, which had the best-tasting cake with fruit in the middle. Funny, I can't remember anything about the vows, but I remember that cake. It has been about fifty years, and I can still taste that cake.

The person who was going to pick me up in my wedding gown was so busy cleaning his car and shining it to look good that he forgot the time and was over an hour late. During the time he waited, Sam was praying, and before I arrived, he told me that he heard God say to him, "If you harm her, I will punish you." Talk about fear. What a way to enter a marriage. I never knew that he had pimped before he found God, and now he would romance anyone he could, and romancing included everything. I was devastated but loved him and also thought I had to keep his life covered as he was now a minister too. He would always ask for my forgiveness after each infidelity, crying and begging. Then we would go to praying, and after a while I forgave him. We would make up and have make-up sex, which was very loving and nice. What a bargain. Surely God would want me to forgive him. It never occurred to me until years later that I was the "forgiving angel" that he would return to whenever he screwed up and wanted to be right with God. He would cry and beg me to forgive him *and* would promise not do it again. I would yield to his plea and forgive him, feeling so good and godly, and everything would return to normal for a while.

Sam and I worked with Sister Leo for quite a while. We did a little of everything, from cooking to teaching. We traveled with a group of the addicts to give their testimonies in churches all over New York State and even to the other states. It was a busy time but money was scarce and travel hard. However, we needed to bring in money to pay for the needs of the work, and this was the only way to get it.

We had a child, a baby girl. Every day of pregnancy was torment, and I even carried a small garbage bag to throw up in. I rode in between the subway cars going to work because I threw up all the way to work. I had morning, afternoon, and evening sickness. I lost over fifty pounds and looked really good, I thought. I fell down a flight of stairs at work and was rushed to the hospital that night to begin the birth process. My daughter was born early, and "God's" reputation was saved as we had only been married for 8 months.. Everything was beautiful.

Mom made the trip to New York to help me for the first weeks of Joy's life. This was the first time that Mom was well, and we had so much fun seeing New York together. Joy was born in a Bronx hospital that was being closed. This was an exciting experience—not! Being induced is not the joy of life, and amid screams and begging for three days and agonizing pain, she arrived, delivered on a kitchen table because all the equipment was already gone. I was throwing up and was told later that I knocked the nurse over because they gave me ether and I went ballistic. When I woke up, I looked so beautiful on this blessed occasion with matted hair and dirty gown.

They brought the baskets around with the babies. There was one who had a whole lot of hair sticking up above the basket. I was wondering who had given birth to that hairy thing when they lifted her up and handed her to me. One look at her and my heart melted with joy. As I looked into that marvelous face, I knew that she was what I'd always wanted. For a while, our daughter kept Sam happy and devoted. He played with her, dancing and singing. We would take her to church nightly. We would lay her on a pew, where she slept peacefully while we ministered or listened to someone else speak. Sam was the type of person who was very emotional. He was a poet, and he wrote beautiful poems about how he loved me that that made me swoon. I loved romance. He was also very generous. He would give the clothes off his body if he saw someone who had a need. He would never fail to give money to someone who was begging. He was always aware of someone who was hungry or in need. I thought this was a wonderful quality and stood behind him in all giving, even when our own finances were a pittance.

My life seemed very satisfying. I loved the times I was in church services, even though I did not understand a word spoken, because it was in Spanish, but spent that time worshiping and reading the Bible. I loved everything I was learning and feeling. This was a time when we looked to God with such enthusiasm that we did not move in this world but in the space where God was. The wonders of God's presence made the work fun, and we would work night and day. God was so satisfying and fulfilling that I was walking in a joy bubble, singing and praising all the time. Religion can be ecstatic.

An opportunity to work in the Community Progress Center in the Bronx was presented. I was selected to head a unit to work with drug addicts and refer them to the hospital for detoxification. We hired eight other guys from the church and told everyone who came into the unit for help that they needed to repent and turn their lives over to God. Many did and went to live in religious centers that had opened. We were in this community center when Blacks were beginning to rally and things were beginning to change. It was a time of upheaval, but I was too busy to notice. I brought my daughter to work every day, and the guys just loved her. They were told that she had to lay in her bassinette sometime during the day.

I met a doctor who worked at the Bronx State hospital. He was in charge of a unit for chemical dependents. He invited me to come and see what was going on there, and I went, thinking I would learn a lot, but at the end of all the sessions where the "hot seat" method was used, I knew that this was not the way I wanted to bring healing to anyone who was addicted. I returned to work with Sister Leo, and God became the focus again for healing. God would touch you and heal you, and all you needed was God. There were many addicts who came into the church, and before long they were praising God and giving testimony of God's power and love. The addicts were told to just look to God and pray, and that was all they needed. Many of them thought they were ready to minister and opened small storefront churches. The other shoe was about to drop!

Chapter 6

Beginning of Heartache

$\mathcal{D}$amascus began to fall apart. After Reverend Rosado died, Sister Leo fell in love with one of the men, who was also an addict but now was living a good life. She ended up marrying him. Sam and I saw that we needed to make a move. We went on the road evangelizing as we traveled westward speaking in churches, going from city to city. We were in the same boat as most of the others who started ministries before they were ready. We arrived in Los Angeles and were able to connect with friends who had left New York. Times were hard and money scarce, and we decided that we had to go to work to be able to live. I had a door open, and because of my degrees, I got a job as a consultant at the main office of a community program. There were many satellite programs, and

Sam got a job in one of them. We were making good money at last. A house, a car, a babysitter, speaking in churches once in a while, and life was smiling all over us. Wow. God was really blessing us now!

One night as we arrived home, he asked me to stay in the car to talk. He said he had been unfaithful again with the secretary of the satellite where he worked. I screamed from the bottom of my toes, feeling my heart breaking from the pain. I can still remember that pain, although it is no longer pain. And again, I forgave him, as he asked, with his promise never to do it again. This time the promise was not kept, and not long after, I came home to find they had been in the house and in our bed. This was all I could take!

I yelled, "You must leave! Get out! I hope God strikes you dead!"

He left, and I went into depression, grieving, crying, questioning why—what was wrong with me? Why didn't he love me? God, what's wrong with me? I couldn't see fault with him, only that I was too tall, too large, too not pretty, and too fat and everything else that made my depression deeper.

Sam called me from San Francisco to say he had gotten right with God and was busy ministering in the streets and churches. He asked if I could come to see him. I did. I registered in a fancy hotel, and he came over to see me and wanted to take me to dinner. We ate in the dining room of the hotel where there was a band playing, and it was all so romantic.

After dinner we were talking, but the music was so inviting and people were dancing, so I asked him, "Why don't we dance?"

"Do you know how to dance?" he loudly asked in total surprise.

I was surprised he did not understand that I also had a life before God took it. We danced, and he was in shock for the whole night. Today as I look back, I have a better understanding of our lives together. Sam only knew me from the church, so he really did not know me at all as a human, and I needed Sam to make me feel beautiful and accepted. I would put up with his unfaithfulness, gallantly showing him God's love just to keep him. Sam was small in structure and could have been a model. His looks were what I wanted, tall, skinny and so good looking. It's too bad we tend to jump into relationships too fast and, before understanding ourselves, become entangled physically and emotionally. But the journey must go on. I did, however, go back alone and told him to continue to seek God.

I got a phone call from a hospital in Las Vegas. My daughter, mother, and father had been in an accident, and they said I should come right away as they did not know if they would live. They might not make it. This shook me to the core. Desperately I drove to the airport to take a flight to Las Vegas. My parents had been taking care of my daughter while I was trying to get myself together. No one mentioned how she was. Was she already dead and they would not tell me? I did not know whether my parents would last till I got there. Frustration and fear held me.

Arriving at the hospital, I learned that my daughter was not hurt because my mother had thrown her body over her and protected her as the car rolled over and over. My mother was horribly hurt and they thought she would not live. My father had been hit in the back and was in horrible pain but was alive and emotional. Alone with my daughter, in my parents' home, I called my husband.

Time brought some healing as both of my parents lived. My husband came to comfort me but I knew he was still involved. I told him to leave Los Angeles and get right with God. I stayed with my parents, who were in the hospital for a long time. My father was released first and my mother months after, as she had to be rehabilitated to walk again. She was in bad shape and suffered the rest of her life from the effects of the accident. I had to return to work. Sam was going on the road trying to find God, and Joy had to come to Los Angeles with me. I found a wonderful woman who babysat while I went to work. On weekends I would go to Vegas to see my parents. I didn't know why God was putting me through such hard trials but was determined to continue to trust. God must be testing me.

After the accident, Mom and Dad moved back to the farm and my grandfather in Minnesota. He was old and sick. He was told that he had cancer of the kidneys and this could not be operated on, so he was to live out his time at home. Mom and Dad moved in with him, and Mom nursed him daily, taking care of all his bodily needs. During this time there was a new relationship built. Grandpa began to love and appreciate Mom. I was in college at the time, but when I came home, I watched the compassion and care my mother had for him. After the way he had treated her, it was a real lesson for me. Mom did not hold grudges even when she was treated unfairly and cruelly. In fact, I never heard my mother say a cruel word to anyone. I knew she had been battered and beaten down, but she just moved along in life doing what she needed to do.

Can you imagine what it is like to be in an earthquake? Lying in bed, I saw the ceiling crack as the bed was swaying. I hurriedly dressed, and taking my daughter, I took the car and drove to the babysitter's house. The streets looked like a bomb had gone off. She informed me that I was a nut driving in the streets with gas flowing from broken pipes. She turned on the television, and I saw for the first time the horrible damage that was done by the earthquake. I was in shock, and fear began to creep into my heart. The office where I worked was shut down and stayed that way for over two weeks, and when it finally opened, we sat at our desks and watched the lights sway in the aftershocks. The vulgar language flowed each day at work, and soon I was using the same language until I caught myself cursing my car. I felt so guilty and had to ask for forgiveness right away.

I was relieved when Sam called and said he had gotten right with God and was working in the upper Minnesota area. He found a person who was willing to sponsor him to start a house for people in need of help. He needed me right away. Would I come as soon as possible? I, of course, rushed with hope in my heart that he had really found God again and he was serving God the right way and would be faithful. I drove from Los Angeles to Minnesota with my small daughter sleeping in the car and with all our worldly possessions. A new chapter had begun, I thought.

We had a lot of kids (it was the hippy generation) live

with us, and we ministered to them daily. A church sold their building to us, and we moved into it and made room for people to live with us. The basement was for men and the Sunday school rooms for the women and us in a lovely add-on with two bedrooms. We began to have services, and pretty soon the church was full of young people. I soon found that I was doing most of the ministering. I knew I had a gift to teach and felt a stirring within me that made me want to always teach and share with others. After being there for several months, I asked Sam why he wasn't preaching very often but was giving the service over to me. He replied that he was going through a dry spot and he would just like to lie back for a while. I accepted his reason and prayed for him.

I was determined to find out how to help Sam get on the straight and narrow, so I decided I would get some help from other ministers. The first minister I opened my heart to asked me, "What is your sin that Sam is living like this?" The second stated that because Sam was married before, we were living in sin and our marriage was not holy. His first marriage occurred when he was on drugs at sixteen. He had divorced her, which he should not have done according to this pastor. He belonged with her, so we were living in sin, and therefore Sam was only showing his guilt at having abandoned his real wife. The third said I could never marry again or minister if we divorced because I had the only opportunity given to me to marry once and only once. This was my future. This wonderful advice caused me not to trust in the doctrines of churches. How could three ministers give different advice from the Bible? "What do You want, God?" I asked after returning home exasperated and confused. The answer came. All condemnation was lifted, and I was free to be me. It did not give me any advice on how to help Sam.

I had been asked to bring some of the girls up to a church about one hundred miles away, and after the service, we returned home right away. I was told by one of the remaining girls, named Patty, that there was a phone call from Sam in which he told her that he was at a motel and she could come over. She was not aware that there was another Patty who was having an affair with Sam, so she was confused at the message and thought that he meant to say Helena instead of Patty. I got the name of the motel, and with fear and my heart beating fast, I went to the,motel and asked for the room number. The door was slightly open and with my foot I touched it slightly and it opened to the view I dreaded. There they were in bed together.

As I walked in, Patty grabbed the blanket, ran to sit in a chair, and stated, "We were just being friendly."

This broke my train of thought, and I began to laugh at her stupidity. "You and your friend can go to hell."

Jaws dropped as I turned around and walked out of the room. Sam did not return home, and I assumed he was staying with Patty, which was right. It was time for me to step up to the plate and make a decision. It was evident that Sam was not going to change now, and perhaps he needed to really learn a lesson, so I divorced him. He did not even show up for the court date, but after he received the outcome, he came to see me and as usual started using "friendly persuasion" to try to get me to forgive him. He now wanted to cheat on Patty with me. Shaking my head, I declined his offer, and then he stated that his only wish now was that we could live our lives together again. Of course, I wanted that too because we'd been married in God, and that would be right.

After Sam left that ministry, I was told that because my head was now gone, I could no longer be in charge of the ministry, and they would be looking for another person. I would have to move on. These people believed that a man had to be the head of any woman in ministry. Sam had been found in a motel committing adultery, and I had been ministering for many months alone, but it didn't matter. There was a doctrine that said that a woman could not minister unless she had a man covering her head. I had to go. Note that all the time that we were there, we did not receive an offering or salary. We had our living expenses, so I was left with a five-year-old daughter, no money, and no place to go. At that time we had about twenty people who came in to find God living there. One of these became a real friend, and we prayed and held the people together. Ten of the others said, "Wherever you are going, we are going too." And so we all began to pray. Joy, my daughter, was by the bed playing and overheard two girls talking about how horrible it was that Sam did this to Helena. She immediately became the taking care of mother person, at age five. She protected me until she was in her teens and looking for a life of her own.

Chapter 7

Beginning a New Path

*I*t's funny how many times prayer has been answered in my lifetime. This was one time it was answered by a phone call from a pastor saying that he had a vision that I came down the Mississippi River in a boat and it came to rest at the Embers Café on Ferry Street in Anoka. I had a Carmen Gia convertible car that had been given to me. It had been in an accident, and the frame was bent slightly. I could drive it but only at 30 mph or 80 mph. Driving eighty all the way from Moorhead to Anoka, we arrived at the Embers and looked curiously over to the house on the river. It was a big stucco and brick house that was seated on a large yard, which had not been mowed for a long time. Walking over and around it, I thought, *God, this can't be You?* But I still knocked on the door and was invited to come inside. There were several guys living there, and they were partying daily. There was a Christmas tree in the living room made of beer cans and black lights all around. The cupboard's door had been torn off to make a bonfire on the beautiful living room wood floors, leaving a horrible burnt stain, there forever. The upstairs toilet had overflowed, and the ceiling in the dining room was hanging down from the wetness. It was damp and cold in the house because there was no heat. The residents could not afford heat. Drugs were much more important.

For some reason, I was compelled to make an offer: "I will give you back this month's rent if you will leave in a week."

I didn't know where or how, but by faith I made the offer thinking, *It will only be until we get somewhere else.* They agreed and left, and I went home thinking, *At least we can go somewhere.* I went to see the owners of this building on Ferry Street and they were in agreement with the plans, but they said it would only be for a short time as they had dealings with a church, who wanted to build a high rise for senior citizens. This fit into my thinking as I thought God would provide another place soon—and did not worry

Moving day came, and there was no money. One of the guys said he had enough money to rent a truck to take everybody's things, so off he went to get it. We packed and moved all of our belongings into the truck. About an hour later as we were cleaning up the remains, I received a registered letter. Inside there was a check from a brother of my grandfather's estate, and with much rejoicing and praising God, I cashed the check, and off we went to Anoka, my daughter of five years, my friend, and the rest of the remaining people. It was a scary move, but God was with me.

The house was large and in much worse shape than I had thought. There was a dog who had lived in the basement and had never been let out—ever! The basement was cement that was covered with mud, and there was a makeshift shower with a hose thrown over a clothes railing. There was an outer room that needed work badly.

The upstairs was broken down with no bathroom that worked but was being used anyway. There were three bedrooms and two porches. The rooms were in pretty good shape, and so the girls all chose their rooms and moved their stuff into them. Joy and I chose the rooms by the porches, which looked out over the river.

Downstairs, the men took the rooms that had some heat and slept in sleeping bags until the windows in the porch could be replaced. They had all been broken out. The house was a disaster! Lucky for us, there was a pastor who was very interested in the work, and his church came to help us make it livable. There were four big truckloads of garbage that were taken to the dump, plus windows replaced and holes stuffed with paper then masking taped over to make it ready for paint. We were able to get some paint donated, and although it was an icky brown, it made the house clean. The bathroom upstairs was repaired and the ceiling torn down, and new plaster board was put up. We were home. It didn't take long before the word was out that we were there and helping the homeless, and pretty soon there were thirty persons living in the house. We lived on food stamps when my money ran out. Everyone donated their money and food stamps, and we were able to keep the house going all through the first winter. We spent a lot of time praying and talking about the Lord's provision, which always seemed to happen just in time. Once a food truck stalled in the driveway and the driver came to the door and asked if we had need for food and could take what he had as his freezer was on the blink and the food would not keep. We all rejoiced, and together we helped carry the food from the truck to our house. We feasted for days. God was good!

There were people from all states who came to

see what was going on at Shiloh. We chose the name Shiloh because it means "peace until Messiah comes," and we wanted to be ready for the second coming. We were having Bible studies each day and thought this was wonderful. The house was little by little being repaired and looking nice. Thoughts that God would supply another place were replaced with thoughts that God had given us this place. To ensure this was true, we marched around the house and through the yard declaring, "This is the house of the Lord."

The owner of the property and building called, and I was informed that the church that was going to buy the property had reconsidered and we now could own it for a sum of $60,000. What a joke! We were living on welfare. Now talk about miracles. A man who I had known came to see me. He was covered with guilt and needed to be told that God would forgive him. He had slipped and done the things he had considered sin. He had been to Las Vegas and had won a great deal of money. He considered it to be dirty money and asked me if I would consider taking it. My heart jumped. I told him there was no money that was dirty when it was for God's purposes. We prayed and wrote out a check for $25,000. I contacted the owner of the building and we made the deal, but this time the property was for $80,000. Shaking I gave him the money I had and then was told how much I had to come up with every month. It was done.

Shiloh was mine Wow! My heart soared as I went home to tell the rest. I had never thought of buying something and for $80,000. This was out of my thinking, but I had done it. "God, please…" help me make the payments! We all had a good prayer meeting with a lot of rejoicing. It was good to see God move.

My personal life was not as happy. Sam had not repented or even called, and I was sure that he would. As time slipped by, I switched from the pain of not having my husband to anger at him for not getting right with God. I then heard that he had married Patty and had moved from Minnesota to California. I religiously committed him to the devil that his flesh could be destroyed that his soul might be saved. I hung onto the hope that he would repent. Wow, what a martyr I was. Then one morning as I was waking I heard in my heart, "Consider him dead," and I knew Sam was gone. It was as if I had been washed of ever knowing Sam as my husband. But I did not know that there was a cleansing I needed. Several days later when I was praying, I heard in my heart that I had to forgive Sam. This was not to my liking as I hadn't done anything wrong, and I fought to the point of being flat on the floor crying for hours, until I yielded. I got up and was going on my way when I heard again, "Now bless him." What, are you kidding? Sure enough, this was for real, and on the floor I went again until I knew that God's love went way beyond what my pea brain could understand. God loved beyond what was seen.

I blessed him and Patty and whatever he would do and anything else I could think of. It was beautiful, and I was free—no pain, no longing, no Sam! With a sigh of relief, I praised God. It was time to get on with my life.

Things were picking up at Shiloh. We had been attending a church all this time because ministers had told me that to be right with God I needed a male head. I began teaching, and that was what I dearly loved. The numbers of the church had begun to really pick up. It seemed everyone wanted to be involved with Shiloh and wanted to attend the Bible studies. Besides studies, we had a hilarious time. We had a group of genuine nuts come all the time, and with that came all kinds of good times. The shackles were taken off, and we began to laugh and tease each other. Life was fun, and serving God was joyful. Little did I know the trial that was ahead.

The pastor of the church we had attended had been kind of standoffish with me, and I knew something was not right. He called me into his office one day, and he and his wife told me that I was no longer welcomed at his church because I was a witch and had bewitched all the people. *I couldn't believe what they were saying.* What was wrong with these people who couldn't see my heart? I sadly went back to Shiloh and shared with all those who were living there what they had said and released anyone who wanted to continue to go to that church. I assured them that they could still live at Shiloh if they wanted to go there. No one wanted to go, so we began our own Sunday services and Bible studies, and a church was born. We called this church Shiloh Ministries and even had it registered by the state. It was destined to begin many different ministries, which through the years it has done.

There were now over forty-five people living at Shiloh. Many came to study with me, and before long we had a Bible school going. There were twenty students. For over two years, we studied and praised and preached and preached and preached. Some of the students were good, and some were boring. My friend asked me to make her husband a copastor, but I did not feel he was ready as he did not show me the compassion I wanted to see before I appointed someone to this position. One Sunday as he was scheduled to speak, I did not realize that I had a mic open on me, and as I listened, I whispered, "Oh, shut up." I was told later that the entire congregation had heard me. Oops! I thought about the scripture in the Bible that states not to give a novice too much power as it may destroy him. I denied this request to make him a copastor. There were so many things that happened during this time that I am not able to include in this book because we would be here for a year. Gifts of the Spirit became the leader, and many followed the words of prophecy. The more one had visions or prophesied, the more one was revered. Instead of love, the gifts became the measure of holiness. Things were out of order, and I could not correct them.

On the agenda of things that manifested was a trip to India. I had been invited by an Indian pastor to come and speak and sing at a convention they were going to have. After traveling half my life (it felt like it), I arrived in Bombay. We had to take an airplane across India to the other side of India. This was another time that God saved my life. The planes rattled and shook, and I prayed. This trip was an eye opener! I had never seen so much poverty. I never thought children in the orphanage could live in one big building and sleep on leaves for a bed, with no other furniture. They were given one bowl of rice with curry a day. This was sponsored by the churches in America. The pastor and his wife lived in a house with refrigerator and a shower and ate off silver plates. We even had showers. We stayed in their house and were given meals with meat. The saris worn by the wife and sisters were gorgeous, with gold mingled through the cloth. Their lives were quite comfortable, which I could not grasp as there was so little given to the people who came to study and the orphans who lived there. One of the children became very close to me. I invited her to come to the house and we could talk more, but she declined, saying, "No, no, that is not allowed." This was hard for me to understand, but I saw the caste system was even in the church.

The convention brought in thousands of people who stayed for all four days of the convention. They slept in the huge tent and all around the grounds. The smell was awful as all the daily needs had to be met in one of the corner of the property. This area was sprayed with Lysol every day, which only added to the stench. They were fed one bowl of rice a day. I learned a song in Swahili and became the hit of the day. The children would fall out laughing when I sang because they had not heard a Westerner (American) sing before. The caste system was very evident, and I could not stand to see inequality. I determined that if I came back, I would sleep and live with the people. I got dysentery in the last days we were in India and was teased that I would end up in the Ganges River. It was a very happy day when I left. I kissed the ground of America when I returned. Yet I learned a very valuable lesson. It was in India that I saw people happy and content with nothing. An excitement of life was in all the children as they followed me every day, wanting to touch me and give me their favorite snack, very hot curried bites. I gave them chocolate candy, and they spit it out with distaste. Other pastors were there too and were quick to add their names to those who started Bible schools or orphanages. They could say that they had a mission in India. I did not care. I would send money to the poor. Soon I had letters coming to me from India asking for support by some person who had gone to the Bible school and was now on his or her own. Word spread to the point that I had to stop sending money altogether.

My daughter did not graduate from high school but went straight to college. She was having some problems about this time and ended up having to get counseling. She was such a beautiful girl and fit into the fast crowd with other models, who were invited backstage at concerts. She hated the person I was going to marry and didn't want to be around him, so she moved out of my house with her boyfriend and enrolled in theater in school, for drama. The leader got arrested for child abuse, and her career ended in that school. Joy got her life in order and told me she was now ready to do modeling. She went to college and got her associate's degree and now was ready for something else. Her look was very exotic and did not fit into the Minnesota scene, so off she went to New York, where she was told that she needed to go to Europe because of her look. On my fiftieth birthday, I said good-bye to my precious daughter, who was bound for Italy. I was crying as I drove home but knew that she had been given to God. I returned home to a surprise birthday party for me at Shiloh.

One of the stories I will not spend much time on is James, who I married. James was an alcoholic. He was a man who was very intelligent, witty, and handsome. He had been abused as a child by an alcoholic, cruel mother, who used him as a target to throw knives. Finally, Social Services placed him in an orphanage when he was just a baby, with the stipulation that he had to keep his father's name and was never to be adopted. He had gone from the orphanage directly into the armed service and there was placed on helicopter duty to go into areas and destroy the villages. He said he got drunk before and after, and that's how he drank. He was mean when he drank, and life with him was not very pleasant. He was a perfectionist, and when things were not perfect, he got drunk. I would listen to drunk logs and stories about when he was in the service and the horrible missions he had to go on killing people until I wanted to get drunk, but I never did. It was time to leave him, which I did. For several years he called me, sometimes fifty times a day. I finally told him that I was going to move to Italy to be with my daughter, and he stopped calling and moved to Texas. James thought he was too sick to be helped because he knew he would be an alcoholic all of his life. Even God could not change him. Giving up hope, he continued to drink.

There were a lot of changes in the wind when I was married to James. My friend had a vision of James in a bed with me. I was turning his head upward so he could find God. She had advised me to marry him because he would find God through me. I foolishly took her vision to be of God and brought James into my life. There were very good times when he was sober and open, mostly after a drunk, but there became more and more times that were terrible.

With my friend's husband not accepted as co-pastor and James's drinking lifestyle, Shiloh split. The young people left me with a vision given to them that I would be gone before the year and Shiloh would fall. See, I told you my life sucked. The funny thing that happened to me at this time is that I didn't feel it was wrong for these people to leave. It was a strange feeling as I felt no anger or desire to make them understand. God had a plan for them and for me that was different from the path we had walked together. I was at peace and inwardly knew God had moved this way for it to happen. Today I look at it and know there had to be a split because there were new things coming down the pike. I had prayed for a deeper walk and this abandonment by my friends brought heartache yet this was the beginning of new understandings. I began to make my way back to the core of life and was awakening from a deep religious sleep.

Left with a handful of people, we had to begin building again. There were several more mature people who stayed because they thought they were foolish. They became the solid ground of Shiloh. There were Leo and Donna, there was Dolly, and there were Dan and Paula. There were Denny and Eileen and John and Sandy and Don and Doug, just to name a few. The ones who stayed were those who joined with me in heart and gave and gave of their time and lives. We had so many good times and thoroughly enjoyed each other's company. There were still the homeless that lived there, and they seemed to grow in numbers each day. A community agency had heard of the work we were doing and came to see if I would like to receive some money for the homeless. They contracted seven beds that they would pay nine dollars for room and board. We thought we had hit pay dirt. We were the first shelter for the homeless in Anoka. Donna and Dolly worked each day cooking and helping the homeless. Donna would go painstakingly through the cans that were donated that had no labels and find out what was in them. Some dog food was found, and we would laugh, teasing that it was going to be served. These cans of donated food were where most of our food came from, with a little donation for meat. We had food, help and God, and then there were many homeless like Peter. We had some very interesting people come to Shiloh

Peter, who lived on the streets because the state hospital had released many of their patients, came often. Many, like this man, ended up living on the street because of the decentralizing program of the hospital for the mentally ill. Whenever he would come to Shiloh, we all were aware of his presence because his smell went before him. Dick, a worker, would hurry him downstairs to the men's section and have him strip off all his clothes, and he was given other clothes to wear until his were washed. I came down to the dining room and did not recognize him because he was so small. His voice startled me, and I saw it was Peter. I asked him why he was so small, and he replied that he wore five coats so he would look big and he would not be beaten up. He would always come for food and even a bed, if we had one available. He kept his cigarettes in a Tupperware box and would barter cigarettes for things. Peter was a loving hoot, and we grew very fond of him. He purchased a sleeping bag and slept under our porch because he felt safe.

His auntie, who had raised him, died, and he came to us to help him. Donna, Dolly, and I decided that we should go to the funeral and give Peter a ride. On the way Peter insisted that we stop at a drugstore where he had seen a statue of an angel that he wanted to place in Auntie's casket. Dolly and Donna had dealt with him a lot and had decided they would not make any stops, but they did. Peter's charm won out, and as soon as they arrived to the funeral, late, of course, Peter went immediately up to the casket and put a letter and the statue into it. And the service went on. We were invited to go to the aunt's house for coffee, and it was there that I was told by another aunt that Peter was born normal but his Father has held him upside down and hit his head against the floor many times and this is why he was mentally ill. We all were sickened when we heard this. It made us love Peter all the more. I have to tell you of a counseling session I had with him. He had come with a very heavy problem that caused him a lot of fear.

He said, "Helena, I have sinned, and I think God is mad at me and I might go to hell." I told him there was nothing he could do that would cause God to send him to hell. He said, "I have had a foreign occasion with one of the girls in the hospital, and I know the hospital would be mad if they found out."

I very seriously looked at him and said, "God loves you regardless of any fornication." Dolly was in the next room and was holding back laughter.

I had always, since living in New York, been interested in seeing numbers, just who, and why, because I had all the years before made a living using the Management Information Systems. I kept track of why people were homeless and found, after a year, that over 95 percent were chemically dependent. I needed to think about this for a while.

About this time my father died a horrible death of emphysema and my mother came to live with me. She was very frail and had to be watched and cared for all the time. My parents had been a big part of Shiloh and came up from their home often just to be with us. Dad brought up a whole truckload of corn, which we had so much fun husking and cleaning to be frozen. We formed long lines for work, and it was like in a factory. We all enjoyed its fruits after. We burned out many electric knives, and our feet stuck to the floor. Mom showed love to all of the homeless and would make them feel good. She would laugh and smile with them and became known as Grandma. Mom never said an unkind word about anyone. She fell one day and broke her leg, making it impossible for me to take care of her. My doctor opened the door for her to go to a nursing home close to Shiloh. Mom was not pleased with this, but I knew she would be safe and was content, except for the food. I would take her out to eat chicken, and she would smile as she ate and sucked the marrow out of the bones. The amazing thing that happened was I began to view her in a different way. Taking care of her made me her frustrated caretaker. Now, when she was in the nursing home I became her daughter, and we had a wonderful time together on my visits. I never realized that she had a sense of humor but it came out there, and I saw how funny and strong she really was. Mom lived in the nursing home until she died. I had been called about thirty times to rush there as she was at death's door. Each time I came and touched her, she revived. I wondered why this always happened.

At a friend's house, I was getting a foot massage from a young man. He seemed rather quiet, but those foot massages were very sweet and good and so was he. When Mom saw Don and they began to tease one another, she liked him and told him to get me. I began to date Don, on the side, for about two years. Finally he told me to make up my mind or he was out of there. I did not want to lose him and was very afraid to get into another relationship, but we became public. I still thought I could ruin God's reputation if things were not perfect and wanted everything to appear okay … We were officially a couple. God, how can you have so much patience with me who is so blind? I thought, *I could ruin* Your *reputation.* How vain can you get. Don became the gift to me from the Spirit. I was given a partner who wanted the fullness of Spirit more than he wanted me. What a find! Another gift to me was my dogs.

Baby, my daughter's twenty-five-pound angora cat, was attacked by a very mentally ill boy, who thought he was making a sacrifice to God. Baby's legs were tied together, and he was thrown into the Mississippi River. After many tears by my daughter and me, we changed from cats to dogs. First, there was Missy, a mixture of cocker spaniel and poodle. Someone had tied him to the clothesline in the backyard and left him there without me knowing it. I kept hearing barking and finally went to the backyard to find this poor, skinny dog all matted, tied to the clothesline. Oh, the poor thing, he looked so miserable. I let him loose, petted him, and took him to the groomer, who shaved him. From that day to his death, he was a wonderful, loving companion with one desire—to make me safe and to love me. Then there was Buffy, a promise made to Joy fulfilled, a miniature white spitz, who looked like a duster. He only lived for several years and died of seizures. Next came Barney, another cocker spaniel-poodle mix. He had been rescued and given to Don. When Buffy died, Barney eased his way into my heart and house. He, like Missy, was my heart.

Then there was Miss Priss, a pom who was destined to go to the hit man, but I got a call and she came home with me. Her name was Sylvia, but when I looked into her eyes I saw a Miss Priss, and she received that name right away. She had been kept in her cage and only let out once in a while to be petted. Someone had taken her voice box out, so when she would bark it was a squeak and a hop. Once out of her cage, she became the queen of the house, and Barney learned to put up with her. Miss Priss died of a blood disease, and I was devastated because I really loved her too. Don made me buy another pom within a week at a dog farm. I got Sam, a tiny pom, who was just a baby. He was sweet and loving and drove Barney crazy because he always wanted to play. Sam was not destined to live long and died in my arms with a heart attack. Again, my heart was broken, but Don began to look for a replacement right away.

That is how I got Beauregard, or Beau. He is another pom who came after a couple of weeks by plane. He was so small but had big feet. Don took him out of the cage and held him while I drove the car. I looked at him and could not stop laughing. Beau heard me laugh, and his little face lit up and he struggled to get to me, which he did. He always follows me wherever I go. He sleeps under my bed and wakes me every morning with kisses. Now why would I put this into my story? Because these animals have taught me a lot. They were never anything but what they were. They always loved, even when they were scolded. They had positive energy greeting me at the door whenever I came home. And there was love that was freely given whenever I needed to be comforted. If this isn't a lesson of what God is like, what else could teach us better? The memories of their lives bring me great joy. They were so cute and loving. Seeing God's love for me in their eyes blessed my heart for many years.

Trying to figure out what I am has been a lifelong journey. For many years I thought and believed that I was a person on earth who needed only to obey the

God who is in heaven, who also was told that He lived in my heart. This understanding never satisfied the yearning that I had for a real experience with God. I enjoyed the hoopla that went with the religious kind of understanding. The praising, singing, and exciting words spoken by the pastor were very comforting; but the need for a more intimate God was calling and drawing me into a deeper walk. There were times when I was speaking and suddenly it seemed that I was a vessel that stood by as something took over and spoke through it. At these times I wondered who knew the things that were coming out of my mouth. Teachings flowed that I had never read about or thought about, but once they were out of my mouth, I had to begin a new way of searching for information.

Chapter 8

Beginning of Wisdom

I was confused by the words in the Bible that seemed to be used in the wrong way. The word *soul* and the word *spirit* seemed wrong in the text. I began to ask God to show me. There was a time before this was revealed. The soul, I saw, was the space between my flesh and the spirit. It is the container of all information that I have heard and experienced and was taught. The soul makes no distinction about what it is receiving, good or bad, and is like a container that can recall all things. If the soul and the body are in connection and they are thinking all things from experiences and knowledge, they can become a force that is insanity. This is the way people are living without a worthy purpose or an ethical way of existing.

The soul is bound to repeat the way of living from what was given to it.

Then there is the spirit. The spirit is what connects us to God, and when this happens, all hell breaks loose. Things believed from childhood are viewed, and they seem to not fit into the life I want. My body, which I always hated from day one, becomes a vessel in which I carry the soul and now the spirit. Every moment there is activity going on inside of me that is contradicting things I thought were right and true. The soul actively questions the new material and sends *out* the message, "You must be having a nervous breakdown. Don't lose control of who you are. Be careful. This could be the devil." The spirit's response is peace.

It took several weeks before there was a breakthrough. It came from the Bible. *For God has not given you a spirit of fear, but one of love, power, and sound mind.* Wow, that was plain. I was not going crazy. I had a sound mind. After that I began to search more for what I needed and came across another quote from the Bible: *When the spirit of truth has come, he will lead you into all truth.* These two scriptures opened my brain, and I was released from the fear of religion. A whole new world was opened to me, and I was confident I would be kept in truth by the spirit of truth. One of the first books I read was written by Jacqueline Small, *The*

Transformers. It was the explosion that my heart needed to begin to look at so many of the memories of my soul and transform them. This, of course, has taken most of the years I have lived. Daily I am searching my soul, and with great compassion the spirit opens the hidden thoughts and brings them into light and understanding.

Completion of the circle of life is the base of all, the spirit, which takes on the soul, which takes on the body. Everything is built on the spirit of life, which turns out to be the reason we are born to flesh in the first place. To experience the life in the flesh and then experience spirit brings us to the reality of who we really are. A spiritual person arises like the Phoenix, which shakes off the ashes of their former lives and reveals the being that is one with spirit, renewed, restored, and reborn.

An extraordinary experience happened to me one afternoon. I had fallen to sleep and began to dream, and as I dreamt, I was in a dream but having a dream. In this dream, I was dancing with a figure I could not recognize but knew intimately. We did not seem to have legs. We were floating in such harmony that I was totally given to the beauty. I longed for that harmony in life and was grieving because I thought I would never have such beauty in this world. Then the dream changed and I was standing on a hill, and there were lines of people who were coming by me. The first was my dad, and as he passed, I saw his fear of dying. I reached out my hand, and it went straight through his flesh into his heart. I felt his heart was full of the fear and was quivering. I took his heart in my hand and stilled it. It quieted. One after another came with their hearts hurting, and I reached into them and their hearts were quieted. There was a group of people who had left in the split. They were on another hill a little distance away standing and looking, and I asked why they were not coming. I was told that they had already received what they would and would not come my way again. I awoke and was in wonder for the rest of the day. I had received a message from the spirit and knew that my life's dance was with it and from this oneness would come healing. God would use me!

An evangelist came to town. What a preacher! My world was turned upside down, and the braces that were on my brains began to loosen. Ultimate reconciliation—whoever would believe that God loved everyone and no one would be lost? Don't we need a hell for those people who don't know God and don't live a "holy" life? Listening to His message, my heart began to expand. Tears of joy ran down my face to know that God loves everyone and would never send anyone to hell. Boy, had I been wrong about God.

My thinking began to change as I went over all the things I had learned and then by preaching was passing on to others. At first I was very timid, but as time went on, I became more and more convinced that evangelical Christianity was only half right. Church attendance was not being a Christian. Prayer and reading the Bible were not at all the end. Things coming from the heart, not the head, with the word and spirit agreeing, was the new way. I loved this change of thinking that took fear of going to hell away totally. In fact, I saw that hell is the life that we live without being conscious that we are one with God. I was learning that life is a journey we all are on, and we are creating our own lives. We can make it hell if we want to or heaven; the choice is ours. Talk about responsibility—but what fun it is. Fear of God's wrath was gone, and the promise that the spirit would lead me to all truth set me free. Reading everything I could get my hands on opened my eyes to begin to see the wonders of God's plan. Chopra's books, Walsh's books, *Conversations with God*, and Tolle's books were the beginning of my learning. These were books that challenged me to open my heart and take the braces off my brains. My love for the life of the spirit grew rapidly. Preaching was no longer a struggle but that was because it was not important anymore that I had to do it all perfectly. The longing to be in the way of the Spirit was the most important thing in my life. Lessons came all the time. It was like having someone there telling me how to live and be an example of the Spirit. Humor became a flow, criticism started to decrease, and a newness of life with energy fueled me.

As I learned, I shared with the people who were coming to Shiloh for church, which became spirituality, and I was so surprised and in shock at what was coming out of my mouth. I came to understand that I came out of God. Wow! "For from Him and through him and to him are all things." And baby, that's me and everyone, even the "bad" ones. Yes, them too. Oh what a God we have! Little by little the Spirit spoke truths to me, and I would speak what I knew to others, and we all grew. I also realized I could not experience right now everything I was learning. This was a day-to-day growing exercise, and my only task was to stay open and teachable and not let past thoughts interfere with what I was learning, as past and future are only an illusion. It broke my heart as I realized I could not be a part of the religious church world again. Everyone I spoke to was telling me that believing that God loved everyone only opened the door to sinning. I knew in my heart that I could only see how great this made God, and instead of sinning more, it revived me to open my eyes to more truth. Who would want to sin when such wonderful knowledge is revealed? "In the morning when I awaken, I will be like thee." What more could anyone want?

Life is so exciting when you know you are connected to the Creator. Each day more and more information comes because the braces on the brains are loosened and old scriptures take on new and deeper meanings and there is no fear to read everything that is available. Why didn't I see this before? Why did it take me so long? I know now that I am a part of God, and I see myself differently. One day, while driving, I began to ask God questions that had been hidden from me for so long. Why did I have to go through all the heartaches from losing Sam and letting myself get messed up with James? Why wasn't I good enough for Sam to love? As I listened, the answer came. "You always looked at yourself as not being beautiful and drew those to you who were sick. As you cared for them and continually forgave them, you felt good and religious, but not beautiful. Now look at yourself and see how beautiful you really are and that you have been created perfect."

"Oh my God," I shouted through tears, "I am beautiful!"

From that day to this, there has never been a negative

thought about my body. Fat or skinny, I am beautiful. Life sure is good without feeling that you're less than. This seems to be the disease that all of humanity is suffering. We believe that to be accepted by the world, we must hide our lack that makes us not enough. I kept the shame of what I thought of myself secret, and even with belief in God, I did not understand that we are all alike and think that if someone knew what was lacking in us, we would be rejected. The fact is that all humanity thinks they are lacking something and are incomplete. Well, we are until we wake up to our completeness. We are a spirit in a body having a human experience. Forgetting who we are brings so much suffering and hurt. Psychologists have tried to bring healing to the body when what people need is a knowing they are spirit, which is perfect. Our body experience or ego is the outward expression that bring all things we have gone through in our lives, good or bad, to form our personality. That is why I have times of sadness, anger, hatred, and all the defense mechanisms. These have protected me and brought me to the place where I have had to decide if I wanted to live after the feelings of the body or the stillness of spirit. This sometimes feels like a yoyo, one day up and the next day down. Living in the Spirit takes *time*, which is for the body side of us. We walk in what we know and experience. We learn by experiencing what is good for us and what gives us pain and suffering. Jesus taught that we are in the world but not of it.

My daughter had met a man, and they wanted to get married. She brought him home, to America, and after watching him and looking him over, I thought he was very nice and would make her happy, so they got married. I was able to go to Italy for the wedding, which was like a trip to fairy land. Four of my dear friends also attended. The reception was held in a castle with doves and fireworks and music playing and many Italian guests as the groom was born and raised in Italy. They looked so happy, and I went home smiling. Several years later, my grandson was born. He was amazing. I had the privilege of holding him and sleeping with him for several weeks as he was a colicky baby and cried all the time. I was in love. He has loved his grammy since he was born. My desire is that he will know who he is and live a life full of wonder. I am going to spoil him while I can. He will have to work out the details of his own spiritual life.

Another teaching came to me while I was dreaming. In the dream there were people who had left in the split. As they walked around looking at the work, they were critical at what they saw. "God would not like this," they said and I felt terrible and began to cry in the dream. I woke up and was still sobbing and had that awful not good enough feeling in my gut. Now what I was doing with my life was being judged, and I wanted only to please. I lifted the covers over my head and determined not to move until I understood where this hurt feeling came from. About an hour or two later, I was taken to my childhood, when I was about five or six. My aunts were sitting at the kitchen table having coffee, and I was under the table playing. They spoke of how bad it was that our family was going to suffer and would never amount to anything or have a good life now that my mother, had a mental problem. The kids will always be affected. The ache was there, and I knew it could not control me anymore. As I said, "No more," I understood that was a lie that had held me for many years and had made me suffer many times and it had to go.

Music has always been such a big part of my life, but during the religious time, the only music I listened to was religious music, and that was with clapping and dancing in the Spirit and worship. I missed out on the whole Beatles generation and many others. I had completely shut out any classical music because I was taught not to love something that would interfere with your love of God. Little by little I began to listen to the magical notes that formed such melodious exotic music that filled my ears and heart. I heard Leonard Bernstein say that his musical creations came after his talent and the vibrations from above crossed, and that opened my small mind to see that all creation came from that same crossing. Miracles happen all the time. I began to pray for that vibration. Worshiping to beautiful music opened the heaven to me. I felt like I was in a dance with the Spirit. One time as I was worshiping, the Spirit lifted me out of the bed, and I stood in space. My arms begin to grow and grow until my arms embraced the whole universe. I got frightened and drew my arms back because I felt that I would just disappear into the realm of spirit. I now know that I am always in the realm of spirit because I am spirit. Music now is in my life, and so is the wonder of the miraculous. I also know that music passes through a person and goes straight to the heart, and the right kind of music with melody lifts your thinking into spirit. I cry when I am touched by the beauty.

Now going back, the homeless who came to Shiloh were in need of a much tighter program than, "Just love Jesus and everything will be okay." I had seen, from the work in New York and from my own experience with Sam, that we are total persons, and unless we are working to get ourselves healthy, our spirits cannot express who we are. Time and again I saw those who loved Jesus fall, repent, love God again, and then fall again. Why? Because loving Jesus is not enough. We must change our way of thinking. The whole person had to be addressed, along with the knowledge of who we really are, and this is the vision that led me to start another work for addicts. I decided that I would get out of the form of religion and needing only Jesus and look into the treatment programs that were state licensed. I hired someone to write the proposal for this to get state approval. For over a year I waited for this to be done, and when I asked them for the evidence, they showed me one paragraph beautifully written but not enough to submit, so I sat down and looked at the outline that was provided by the Department of Human Services and wrote day and night for three weeks. The proposal was submitted and approved. The next step was getting the license. I needed a letter of needs given to me by the county indicating that there was a need. Talk about being turned into a villain in a short time. The council did not want me or a facility for addiction. They wanted to own the ideal property that Shiloh was on, by the banks of the Mississippi River on a large yard. I was informed that the city council had plans for the property before I came along. However, I could not figure out why they did not buy the property when the price was low. I had to be approved by the state, and that was how I opened Transformation House.

Thank God for the wonderful people who shared the vision. They were there always encouraging and helping. We worked and rejoiced to watch clients change their lives. Don, my sweetie, was the first cook and prepared meals fit for a king. Donna became the first tech, and she and her husband moved into a facility to be the live-in staff. Dolly also became a technician and worked until she was tired and retired. Some of the people who were with me left as their families grew and new places for their children were necessary. Many still remained supporters even though they did not want their children around addicts. Shiloh Church became the church for addicts in recovery, although other people who are not drug or alcohol addicts always attend. These wonderful friends know that addiction is not only for those on drugs and alcohol but anyone who has not been awakened to his or her true self. They have supported the program for years. Thank God for their faithfulness.

My daughter and son-in-law moved to the United States from Italy. He is now working for me and is bringing in a new way of seeing and doing things, which I think will improve many of the problem areas. My daughter is looking over what is going on so she will be ready when she is needed. I am learning to keep my mouth shut and am trying to listen instead of instruct. I guess I am quite stubborn at times. This is an area the spirit has not dealt with yet. All in all, it is a growing time with family, and I think I will live through it.

Don has been a constant. I have learned to trust him, although I swore I would never trust a man again. He teaches me patience as he teaches me love. There has never been anyone who would put up with a headstrong, stubborn woman like me, but he does. He looks at me and states that he sees God in me, and that is why he loves me, and we live together; he sees all good and bad. Through thick and thin, he was there to pick me up when I was down, to rush me to the hospital when I am having some horrible illness overtake me, to scold me when I eat too much sugar (I am a diabetic too), and so many more indescribable things. We read together and discuss what we read, which is such a blessing for me because I give teachings and groups on spirituality daily. I am so lucky. I used to look at couples who seemed happy with such envy, but now I enjoy the relationship I have, even in the bad times, and enjoy learning to live as a spirit in a body

Through the seventy-eight years of my life, I have witnessed many things that have happened in the world. The role of woman has been opened, which has allowed me to be the person God intended me to be openly. Wow, how good is this! Religion has also opened, and new things are being taught and allowed that in my day were not possible. People are demanding more than a rigid form of religion that does not bring love to the world. Movies and songs are being written that reveal that the Spirit is inside everyone. There are so many books being written that are opening the minds and hearts of people all over the world. The Spirit is moving, and although it seems small and slow, it is powerful, even though it is not a visible phenomenon. Those who are awake are seeing the tide roll in and rejoice. In the movie *The Lion King* the message is, "Remember who you are." The message is going throughout the world in many forms. The Great Spirit in each of us is yearning for fulfillment. The greatest lesson of life is finding out that God's love is *not* conditional. Regardless of what we have done or what we are doing, God loves us. And further, love is God, which is what we are to be to the world. Our oneness with God makes us the instrument of visible expression for the invisible.

Yet in the world things go on as before, with greed being the leading and most popular human trait. Kingdoms have fallen, only to have new kingdoms rise, and more and more the rich get richer and the poor are a growing number. Besides all the wars and uprisings in other countries, here in the United States there has been a considerable rise in the use of drugs. New more dangerous drugs are being manufactured in garages. The war on drugs has been lost. Those who used heroin or cocaine now use these drugs plus other drugs and put them into their bodies to get the best high possible. This has placed many addicts in danger, and through the years I have witnessed many vibrant young people die of overdoses and other drug and alcohol reactions. The policy of the government has been to put them in prisons, which has turned into a nightmare, as there are just not enough jails or prisons to hold them. Then the mixture of different persons in jail for many diverse crimes, from murder to all kinds of social crimes, is producing a new race of criminally minded people. I have found that we are treating a sicker population now. These addicts cannot change without a program that does not reach into the depth of a person and bring healing. Addicts need a program that will change their lives from the inside out. By providing a safe place where a person, without judgment, can look at his or her thinking and behavior patterns and find the ones that have kept them prisoners, hurting, and damaged, they can be healed. A change of their lives means they are living full lives with whole healthy thinking and behavior. This takes time as the whole person has to be dealt with.

As of today, the persons controlling the finances for a program also determine the amount of time given for a person to rehabilitate. Many times these persons have never dealt with drug addicts. The only way to accomplish changing someone is to go to the base of his or her being and introduce him or her to the spirit that his or her body holds. This is who he or she is, not the body that will go to the grave, but the Spirit that has come directly from the *Creator.* Will the governmental agencies ever acknowledge this? And so the struggle to help addicts continues with the same program with just a few minor changes so others will think they know what they are doing. God alone is not the answer. A person is body and Spirit The body needs all kinds of healing, emotional, physical, and psychological, but if this is all, we have only done a half job. Introducing the Spirit while healing the body gives an addict hope. I am more than a body. This is good news. Good news is that they are loved unconditionally regardless of what they have done. The Spirit is moving and we have to go with it.

Unfortunately, the forces that be are not on this

page and keep changing things that do not make a difference but are required. Paperwork is the big thing! If the paperwork is not correct, the program goes on probation. The actual work that is being done in the client's life is not looked at, and they are not aware of what is happening because the chemical addiction problem is growing, and more and more people are in need of help. I believe those programs that are small and intimate will be replaced by big business one day because it is all about money. I have seen so many changes in the field since I was nineteen years old working in the Bronx. There are few programs that have made a difference. Thank God there are those who work from the heart and have changed lives too! Until the powers that be are able to see the whole person and their needs, there will be little change.

If you don't like what you are reading, I will not be offended if you think I am a little crazy. I am seventy-eight years of age this year, and I now express what I want to. I'm a spiritually liberated woman and I have a lot more to say.

Chapter 9

The Ultimate New Beginning

Now as far as my spiritual journey today, I am still open and changing. I am shocked at how many lies and other negative things have been revealed to me by the spirit. I have stuffed a lot of feelings and thoughts into my subconscious mind. I remind myself that there is more truth to come and not to be disturbed. It takes time to be what I want to be. Knowledge, then experience, is the system that brings change. I am yearning for the fullness of Spirit when there is no stinking thinking to filter my thoughts through. One day I will only know the wonder of love. Then, one of these days the real me will disappear and only my old, dead body will be around but only for a little while. Remember it is only an old, dead body that has served me well. Now, rejoice with me. I am a spirit and have gone back into the Creator. This is where I have longed to be all my life, so I will dance as one with all creation.

About the Author

Helena Ana Young was born in the late 1930s to a Swedish family in rural Minnesota. Her life was greatly influenced by her mother, who loved music, dancing, beauty, and God, even though her mother's life had been disaster. She was musically talented, and doors opened for her to go to New York to study for the opera. Experiencing that God existed changed the direction, and her journey with God placed her in a path that brought her to Spanish Harlem, where she was placed in the hands of Reverend Leoncia Rosado, who taught her to love the drug addicts. She did this work until she was married and she and her husband traveled teaching and preaching throughout the United States. Her world fell apart in California when God put her into the school of pain and sorrow that transformed her again and brought her in another direction. She founded a work for the homeless, then founded a church, then founded a treatment center, all the time growing in the knowledge of Spirit. Today she has four treatment centers for persons who have lost their life's direction and have given themselves to chemical addictions. Hundreds have heard a word that has opened their hearts to walk the spiritual path.